Magic in the In Between

Rebecca Barton

BookLeaf Publishing

Presentation by *BookLeaf Publishing*

Web: www.bookleafpub.com

E-mail: info@bookleafpub.com

ISBN: 9789357444644

First edition 2022

DEDICATION

To those still discovering who they are.

ACKNOWLEDGEMENT

I want to thank my family and friends, who have always believed in me. Without them, I'm sure this book would never have happened. Particularly, I'd like to thank Elizabeth for being a sounding board and convincing me that these poems were worth bringing into the light.

PREFACE

The world is a scary place, and when you're not sure of your directions, it can be made scarier still. I believe that life happens for a reason, and in the end, you will find that things that didn't go your way will lead to surprises you could never have hoped to imagine. But in the moment, knowing things will eventually become what they're meant to be is a poor comfort. *Magic in the In Between* looks at all of the moments where life can feel like it is ready to spit you out with no hope left, but if you look closely enough, you can find the glimmer of magic ready to change things for the better in the end.

prologue.

I don't know why the city sound relaxed me. Maybe it was because cities are never where anything happens in my books.

Nothing spectacular ever happened among the concrete walls of human habitation. It was sitting in the cool serenity of a forest basking in the warm feel of nature that magic occurred.

Sitting on a bench in the middle of a city, I was safe.

Nothing ever happened to upset a city.

The hustle and bustle left no time for imagination. The newness of it all held no ancient judgment or wisdom.

In the city, everything simply was.

It is only when the silence has time to eat you whole that the world can take on new shapes, and those shapes have the potential to upset the carefully constructed balance that is necessary for a moment of pretended calm.

calling.

Purpose is what guides you and makes you
But what happens when purpose is lost?
When you're adrift and have no direction
And would do anything, no matter the cost

If only you could find your calling
A path through the unknown and strife
A way to make a mark and a difference
A meaning in the whirlwind of life

But what if your life has no meaning
Your purpose is simply to exist?
How do you take one step then another
Knowing that all that there is ... is this?

A person may seem like a home
A city can distract and divine
But the magic of getting to create your
own path?
That is the world's biggest lie.

whisper.

Snowy hills and barren trees.
If I listen closely I think it's whispering to me.

Birds fly through a clear sky.
A whisper—and a sigh.

The world is transformed, a new day begun
But before I can understand the crunch under
horses' hooves
The new world is gone
Melted, and whispering something new.

choose.

Choose, darling, choose.
You can't have it both ways.

Choose, darling, choose,
Time is slipping away.

You can choose safety or passion,
But darling, it's rough
Because logic and dreams, they never are one,
So choose, sense or love?

A safe little cage that binds you away
Or freedom that casts you to uncertain days
My heart and my brain: Two warring kingdoms
And I'm left on the battlefield broken in pieces
With no clear victor; no clear decision to say

But choose, darling, choose
The sun is fading away.
Choose, darling, choose
Your heart or your brain?

Your head will say,
"there's a clear path to choose."
But your heart will beat faster,
"we've nothing to lose."
So take a firm stance, and take the first step,

And hope the choice that you've made
isn't one you'll regret.

hidden alleyways.

I like hidden alleyways and whispers of
worlds before

Around every corner a hint of what could
be in store.

The pavers speak, the ivy weaves, and buildings
come to life

With promises, and dreams, and "I love you"s in
the night.

vipers.

All I want is to walk the city streets and take in the lights around me

But I can't walk alone, and I have no one I want to walk beside me.

So instead of blissful, reflective solitude

I return to a den of vipers

Where nothing is as it seems and uneasy silence abounds

And a nightlight only multiplies the suffocating shadows around.

words within my mind.

The world is dark and silent.
But the crickets chirp and interrupt my attempt to remove myself from the world.
They are an annoying and persistent reminder of the world outside my car windows.
I can't turn off the world.

If I sit in exactly the right position, my rear view mirror blocks out the street lamp ahead of me.
But the position is cramped, and I long to rest.
But when I do, I find myself blinded as the warm yellow glow of the street lamp makes itself a dagger that stabs from my pupil straight through to my brain.
You would think this blinding pain would help block out the world, but it only brings it into further relief.

The repetitive whir of machinery switches on and off.
Who could be doing something this late? Why aren't they in their homes?

I want to tune out the world, but not the world at large. I want to tune out the world I've constructed around myself.

When did the bricks become playing cards? Why can't I keep my walls intact, where they can keep me safe from the unknown?

Who truly needs to grow? I will stay here, safe in my two-door car, and try to block out the noises that seem to grow every moment.

A wind chime calls. A person walks. All I want is peace, and even alone I can't escape the words within my own mind.

caged.

Have you ever felt like your ribs were a cage? Like if you could just break free of them, you could be so much more.

You could reach new heights and become and understand what has never been before.

You could shape the world to your liking if only you had the ability to embrace what was hidden inside you and bring it out into the light.

stairs.

The stairs creak, heralding my arrival to anyone who would listen

But no one is listening because no one is looking.

And I return to an empty room in an empty home full of people and love that I cannot take part in and have no place among.

Relegated to a tiny corner, pristine and proof that no matter of organizing the world around me can help the chaos in my soul.

ravens.

The ravens flock here.

Their gazes never waver.

For whom their omen?

mediocrity's muse.

The world's not full of adventure.
So it's true, you get what you get.
It's time to settle and stop looking for more.
Because that's how you live and forget.

If you accept what you have then you're drifting.
But it's better to drift than to drown.
Sure you'll never touch starlight or find who
you are,
But you won't get lost if you stay on the ground.

So look forward, and onward, and don't make
mistakes
Keep on the path that you're heading and don't
deviate.
For the paths that are branching could lead to
new heights,
But more often than not you'll just fall to endless
nights,

And it's better to stay mediocrity's muse
Then to bet it all and to lose.
...And chances are that you'll lose.

fairy tales.

I won't read my child fairy tales
So they know the magic wood
Read of hopes and dreams and fairy dust
And things magic, true, and good

They won't see fairies on their doorstep
Or know the power of three
Whispering wind is just wind alone,
And a tree is just a tree.

No dragon will plague them,
No creatures in the dark,
No magic-filled gemstones,
No epic quests on which to embark.

Because the most magic part of stories
Is their power to make you believe.
To see the beautiful in the ordinary,
And from all hardships have reprieve.

But to believe is to want more
To think magic could abound.
And that lie is the fairy tales' most
haunting villain:

The lie that there are fairy tales to be found.

city.

I've never understood people who couldn't feel nature in the city.

It's everywhere.

Its hustle and bustle hides the teeming magic within it, just below the surface.

And while it may be easy to look at all the magic of the city and say that your own life isn't fair.

In truth, that is the magic of the city.

Magic is everywhere, and whether or not it is fair, it is there.

All you need to do is feel the risk ... reach out ...

And take it.

who.

My dream is to be what I thought I could be
before I gave up.

I often wonder what I would do if no one
expected me to be me.
If I knew no one, who would I choose to be?

Who would I be if people didn't need me to
be me?
Who would I be if I could be anything I wanted?

adrift.

The kinds of words that flow in and out of my head when I'm locked inside of it aren't the pretty, cathartic words of venting.

They're the cyclical, rising-tide of a whirlpool; An echo chamber repeating my insecurities back on me until the minutia becomes a shout becomes an inescapable wail screaming for permission to become even more as I become still less.

It's not the words that take you past an imagined hurt.

It's the words that whisper, insidious, claiming that the tiniest parts are right and everything else is wrong and cannot be as it seems.

It's pretensions and a vicious cycle that only serves to swallow me deeper into my own mind. Sinking its claws a little deeper as it refuses to release me from its hold.

A whirlpool in the middle of an endless ocean where I, adrift in a sea of uncertainty, can find no land in sight and can hardly breathe in a cool breath before I am once again gasping through water as I desperately try to write fast enough to block out the sound of my own mind.

silence.

A wind chime rings
Uneven footsteps stagger.
A gate swings open
with a single high-pitched scream.
Three knocks ring out, solid.

Silence.

Don't they know the silence isn't
fooling anyone?

stars.

I had such lofty dreams once upon a time
I was going to reach for the stars and make
them shine.
But the stars turned out to be a little too far,
And I couldn't make myself take a risk that
might leave a scar.

So now I sit staring at the ceiling
Laying down in my bed all alone.
Staring at the ceiling that blocks out the stars
And trying to imagine that I could ever feel at
peace in the place I call home.

But I breathe deep and force my head to clear
Push my way off of the bed.
If I move to the window, I can still find the stars.
And maybe one day I'll even reach for them
again.

complacency.

I've always had too much difficulty doing what I want.

Fear of the unknown has been a constant companion, one my mind disguised as caution and forethought.

I imagine every way that something can go wrong, all of the possible failures and the failures they would in turn cause.

I want to do so many things,
But my mind won't let my spirit take wing.

Complacency.

My mind sees complacency and turns its ugly monotone into pretty dazzling hues, meant to dazzle and only that.

Beneath the pretty surface that I have created for myself, a surface that I have built carefully into a believable facade, one that I can explain to others in peppy tones and sincere thought.

Beneath this beautiful reflection and beyond the perfect wall is ...

Nothing

No, not nothing

Emptiness.

There is nothing in these pursuits I have pursued

My passions are not fulfilled by sweet nothings that are not sweet.

I am empty like the house I have built for myself.

There is nothing for me here, and so I must go.

But I won't.

I've always had too much difficulty doing what I might really want.

fin.

The city is alive, you can smell magic in the air
I breathe in, and realize I finally have decided
not to care.

I've given over ruling my life to me
Forgetting the battle of others' insecurities.

I don't care what they think, I care what I do,
And if it's to my own self whom I am true
Then I'll change as I need, and stay as is fit.
And if others don't like that? I don't care one bit.

My worries will float away like a dove
And I'll find that I, myself, am worthy of love.

in between.

I can only write in a particular mindset.

It's so much easier to write when everything seems wrong.

Because in the times when you feel happy,

Those are the experiences with magic you want to live through.

The in between times are the ones you want to work through.

butterflies.

Sitting on a bench in the middle of the city, I couldn't help but think of the peaceful serenity I felt surrounded by sounds of construction and traffic with an occasional chirp from a bird close enough to be heard but far enough not to be seen. I took a deep breath and felt my anxiety flow away, the creeping sense of dread that I had felt since lying alone in the silent dark of my apartment finally began to release its clutches around my heart and my stomach, and the butterflies that had been threatening to explode left to visit some less fortunate soul.

I don't know why the city sound relaxed me.

www.ingramcontent.com/pod-product-compliance
Lightning Source LLC
Chambersburg PA
CBHW051752130826
49812CB00033B/1115

* 9 7 8 9 3 5 7 4 4 4 6 4 4 *